Wh

MW01226123

"Sometimes I endorse books and other times I endorse authors because I know that whatever they write will be valuable. In this case I can do both. Dr. Karen is a respected colleague and has become a good friend as well. She practices what she teaches and she's a substantial teacher. Power Conversations is a book that makes it easy for you to learn and remember the skills that connect you with others. My mantra is: It's not who you know that counts. It's who is glad that they know you that matters most. These skills will make others glad they know you."

Jim Cathcart, speaker/author of the bestsellers *Relationship Selling*, *The Acorn Principle* and *The Self Motivation Handbook*.

"I am very excited about Dr. Karen Jacobson's book Power Conversations. The primary key to success in any endeavor whether it be personal or in business is the ability to communicate effectively. She has broken down the steps how to have powerful conversations in easily understood tips. These tips can be applied immediately by anyone to achieve strong connections. I highly recommend Dr. Karen's book to anyone who is wanting to expand their influence and relationships to have a greater impact!"

Gary Barnes, President Gary Barnes International, High-Performance business and sales coach, International speaker and #1 Amazon best-selling author.

"Awesome tip book for enhancing communication skills. Great read! The best thing is that you can apply these tips to your daily life. Unlike many other "tip" books, this one is actually interactive and makes you think. I was rather surprised with how much information I learned while reading it and also what we typically take for granted. It's an excellent book that breaks down simple points of communication from a complex web of interaction to simple strands and to practice techniques that sometimes we all forget- Must have book for every working professional!"

Dominick Nardone CEO Saviar, INC, management consulting - holding company

"The doctor is IN! Whatever your communications style is, Dr. Karen Jacobson has the perfect prescription to elevate your skills to the next level. Communication is a big part of leadership, so reading this book will give you the tools to communicate with anyone...and have fun doing it!"

Jeffrey W. Hayzlett, Primetime TV & Podcast Host, Speaker, Author and Part-Time Cowboy

"Relevant, direct and to the point. There is useful information for anyone regardless of the level of your communication skills. Power Conversations is filled with ideas, tips and strategies that are easy to follow and can be implemented immediately. If you are looking to elevate your business or your personal relationships while mastering high-performance communication skills this book is your "how to" guide!"

Elizabeth McCormick, Former US Army Black Hawk Pilot at Pilotspeaker.com, Motivational Speaker specializing in Sales & Leadership

HIGH-PERFORMANCE TRIAD SERIES

POWER CONVERSATIONS:

CREATING FIRST IMPRESSIONS TO LASTING CONNECTIONS

Dr. Karen Jacobson

JONES MEDIA PUBLISHING

Jones Media Publishing
10645 N. Tatum Blvd. Ste. 200-166
Phoenix, AZ 85028
www.JonesMediaPublishing.com

Printed in the United States of America

ISBN-13: 978-1-945849-46-6 paperback

Contents

Physiology

Phraseology

Inner Conversations

Power Conversations

Non-Face-to-Face Communication

Networking

"Communication is a skill that you can learn. It's like riding a bicycle or typing. If you're willing to work at it, you can rapidly improve the quality of every part of your life."

—Brian Tracy

Introduction – Why This Book?

The second half year of kindergarten is a total blank. My mom, my sister, and I got on a 747 Jumbo Jet and had flown across the Atlantic to join my dad and two brothers and moved to Israel. It was a new country, new customs, new people, and most importantly, a new language that I didn't speak. I wanted to make friends, so I had to learn their language.

Little did I know, that decision would shape the course of my life. Israel was a melting pot, and there were people from many different countries all needing to co-exist. In order to connect and communicate with them, I had to learn about them, their habits, and their language. Finding commonalties with people was a key.

After high school I served in the Israeli Military Intelligence as a noncommissioned officer and learned to embrace a whole different style of communication. My position offered the opportunity to work with people up and down the chain of command, as well as with my own team.

After my service I returned to the US and became a chiropractor. One of the greatest gifts was the privilege of taking care of families and, at times, several generations of the same family. In doing so I sometimes had to "talk people off an emotional cliff," resolve conflict, and develop my active listening skills.

You might be wondering what all that has to do with you or even with this book. In a word — Everything. It's the reason why I wrote the book.

In today's business world, communication has taken the front seat. From team building to effective leadership, your ability to connect with people will either propel your career forward or leave you behind. Companies now are more focused on understanding different communication styles, habits, behaviors, in addition to emotional intelligence. Leadership today revolves around people skills and relationship building rather than just job competency.

While many communication skills are common knowledge, they're not always common practice. It's not about being lucky—it's about taking action. What gives High-Performance Communication its edge is that it takes into account both parties in the conversation and offers you strategies to communicate with anyone at any time, regardless of the person's habits, personality, or experience.

I have compiled a book filled with information and communication skills I have learned over decades of study and experience. I packaged these skills in a way that's easy to learn, apply, and make habit.

All you need to do is take one step at a time and be consistent.

Are you ready to uplevel your communication?

Have fun with it!

Communication Basics

"The basic building block of good communications is the feeling that every human being is unique and of value."

—Unknown

Tip 1: The VAK of Communication

Every second we're bombarded by input of information from the environment. We mainly use three of our five senses when observing and perceiving the world around us. These senses—visual, auditory, and kinesthetic—abbreviated as *VAK*—are considered our representational systems.

Visual—what you see

- You're easily distracted, so you must sit at the front of the class and close your eyes to remember things.
- You like charts, pictures, mind maps, and receiving written praise.

Auditory—what you hear

- You like to talk, including self-talk.
- You're often extroverted and can't focus when it's noisy.
- You love books on tape, live discussions, debates, and music.
- You prefer verbal praise.

Kinesthetic—what you feel

- You like to move around and participate in activities.
- You try new things and learn through experience.
- You talk with your hands and prefer close proximity when talking.

What's your preference? _____

Tip 2: The "It Factor"

Have you ever seen someone walk into a room and immediately capture everyone's attention? Perhaps it was a business meeting, a networking event, or a stage performance. That person had a commanding presence, which be called the "It Factor."

What gives an individual the "It Factor"? Here are five things you can practice to increase your "It Factor":

1. Have a made-up mind. Know your *why*, yet still be open and flexible.
2. Be comfortable in your skin. Practice good posture, foster calm energy, and dress for success.
3. Be charismatic. Exude confidence without arrogance—being humble goes a long way.
4. Show genuine interest in others and be approachable. You're not the only one in the room.
5. Know who you are and be yourself. People will see right through you if you're inauthentic.

Tip 3: I Know You Hear Me

Listening is fundamental in building rapport with others. We all have bad habits that can cause us to break rapport and lose the connection with the other person.

What bad listening habits do you have? Complete this brief self-assessment to find out:

- ❑ Do you interrupt the speaker?
- ❑ Do you jump to conclusions or become judgmental?
- ❑ Do you make up your mind before all the information is presented?
- ❑ Do you show impatience when a person speaks at length?
- ❑ Do you start thinking about your responses while someone is talking?
- ❑ Do you start talking about your own experiences and their similarities to the speaker's?
- ❑ Do you ignore nonverbal cues?

If you answered *yes* to 4 or more of the questions, your listening skills could be improved.

Tip 4: Are You Really Listening?

There are three different levels of listening, and each one creates a higher level of engagement.

Disengaged listening—not listening, pretend listening or partially listening
- A disengaged listener will be staring into space, distracted, looking at his or her phone or show complete apathy.

Passive focus listening—focused on speaker (undivided attention), interpretive (understanding)
- A passive focused listener will pay attention, look at the speaker, nod a few times, or perhaps say a-ha periodically, but doesn't provide much dialogue.

Fully active listening—interactive (asking questions), engaged (full dialogue, feelings and ideas exchanged)
- A fully active listener will use different skills to show interest in the speaker and build rapport. These listeners employ a natural mix of visual, vocal, and verbal responses to create engagement.

For more info on listening habits read:
https://drkarenjacobson.com/blog/good-listening-habits

Show you're interested - listen more, speak less

Tip 5: The 3 Ps of Communication

For many years the most popular communication model was based on Dr. Albert Mehrabian's formula, which uses the three modalities of visual (55%), vocal (38%), and verbal (7%) as the standard. This formula is directed toward expressing an emotional response. (See Dr. Mehrabian website http://www.kaaj.com/psych/smorder.html)

In today's world we focus on whole-brain communication, incorporating all three modalities to stimulate both right brain creativity and left brain analysis.

The language aspect of the High-Performance Triad is summarized in the following three pillars: personality, physiology, and phraseology. In other words, who we are, what we say, and how we say things.

The three pillars serve as the foundation for all of our communication, both face-to-face and indirect (i.e., not face-to-face).

3 P's of Communication

Physiology

Phraseology

Personality

Notes

_____

_____

_____

_____

_____

_____

_____

_____

_____

_____

Personality

"To effectively communicate, we must realize that we are all different in the way we perceive the world and use this understanding as a guide to our communication with others."

—Anthony Robbins Unlimited Power: The New Science of Personal Achievement

Tip 6: Who We Are

Ultimately, different people require different strategies to process and assimilate information. These strategies mostly relate to the way we see the world. Our character, our beliefs, and our experiences affect the way we relate to other people and how we present ourselves.

Some of the ideas and thoughts that shape us are as follows:

- *Global Thinking*. Being at cause and in charge of your life vs. at effect where stuff just happens
- *Social Interaction*. extroverted and outgoing vs. introverted and preferring to be alone
- *Decision Making.* Logical and critical thinker vs. feeler who goes with their gut
- *Social Positioning*. Leader who will take charge and control vs. follower who waits for direction
- *Values.* Innovative, out-of-the box thinker vs. traditional, old-school thinker
- *Mindset.* Positive, glass half full vs. negative, glass half empty

- *Attitude.* Confident, we can make it happen vs. insecure, I don't think we can do it

Learn about others and relate to their view of the world

Tip 7: Loner or Crowd Lover?

We don't all behave the same in social settings and in how we relate to others. Some of us thrive in large crowds, while others are quieter. We typically classify people as either introverted or extroverted. For the most part, while we choose to divide society into one of those two groups, they represent the extremes. A large percentage of people fall between those two extremes. And there's also a new category in town: the ambivert.

- *Introverts* are quiet and not very expressive, and prefer small groups or solitude.
- *Extroverts* are animated, dynamic, and outgoing. They love excitement and large crowds.
- *Ambiverts* have a balance of both introvert an extrovert and adapt to situations.

Are you an introvert, extrovert, or ambivert?

_____

Tip 8: What's Your Style?

In conversation, different people will focus on different things. While some of us may be very people oriented and focus on feelings and emotions, others might be more fact oriented and focus on the process at hand. By the same token, you'll find that some people are big idea people and quick action takers, while others need a lot of specifics and require time to digest the information before they can take action.

While we all possess different qualities and can adapt to situations, we do have a general preference that drives our communication style.

You may be familiar with personality assessments like Myers-Briggs Type Indicator® (MBTI®), StrengthsFinder®, and DISC® (Dominance, Influence, Steadiness, and Compliance®). Let's take a general overview, based on the above parameters, and look at some characteristics of the different styles.

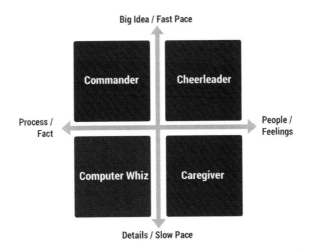

Take your personal assessment at https://drkarenjacobson.com/assessment-tools/

Tip 9: The Commander

If you're a big-idea person who is process oriented and driven, and you want fast results, your primary style is the Commander.

Think of a military commander. You are goal oriented and direct in your approach. You're a no-nonsense man/woman, and you strive to get straight to the point. Nothing stands in your way.

You're a high achiever and will often find yourself in leadership positions. At times you prefer to work on your own because you know the job will get done properly.

You're organized and focused on the facts. You have no time for drama and emotions. It's not that you don't have emotions; there's simply no room for them, since there's much to be done.

The dominant question that drives you forward is *what?* What's next? What's our goal? What needs to be done?

Tip 10: The Cheerleader

If you're a big-idea person who is people oriented and competitive, and you want fast results, your primary style is the Cheerleader.

As the Cheerleader you're animated, expressive, and outgoing. You love working with a team and being with large groups of people. Your main priority is the team itself.

Since you're competitive, you'll often find yourself taking risks, even when unnecessary. You love to share your feelings and emotions to connect with people. Sometimes you can get distracted and have a short attention span.

You're innovative and think outside the box. You do your best. However, if someone takes credit for your work, that person had better watch out!

The dominant question you must have answered is *who?* Who's involved? Who's that person? Who's going to show up to the party?

Tip 11: The Caregiver

If you're a detailed person who is people oriented, and you take your time before you act, your primary style is the Caregiver.

Think of a nurse and caregiver. You're devoted to the rest of the team. You're a great listener who cares about helping other people with their issues.

You're a peacemaker and want everyone to be happy. Therefore, you avoid situations that may lead to conflict.

You're methodical in your approach, and there must be a reason for things. You like tradition and doing things the way they've always been done. You're not a big fan of change, since it disrupts the peace. You're loyal and will stay with a company for years. You love building and nurturing relationships.

The dominant question that occupies your thoughts is *why?* Why should we change things? Why can't we all just get along? Why don't you let me help you with that?

Tip 12: The Computer Whiz

If you're a process-oriented person, focused on facts and details, who needs time to analyze before you make decisions—and the results must be perfect—your primary style is the Computer Whiz.

Think of an analyst or an engineer. You're factual, direct, and thorough in your approach. You're practical, and things need to be logical and flow in the right order. You're reserved and prefer to work independently, staying in the process.

You have high standards, but you're low risk, and you seek perfection, which at times slows you down. In addition, these characteristics will steer you away from changes, especially when the methods haven't been proven.

The dominant question that moves you forward is *how?* How will this process work? How will we get this done? How can we incorporate this into our current process?

Tip 13: It's a Personality Conflict

Depending on your style, you'll get along with some styles better than others. We generally get along with people we have something in common with. A Commander who is process oriented will get along well with the Computer Whiz. The commander will also get along with the Cheerleader, because they are both big-idea/ fast pace people.

As mentioned above the Cheerleader gets along with the Commander. The Cheerleader also will get along with the Caregiver, because they're both people oriented.

We already know the Caregiver will connect with the Cheerleader but they will connect with the Computer Whiz as well since they roll at a similar pace.

Challenges arise when we seemingly don't have anything in common. That's when conflict erupts, because we operate and communicate in the opposite way of the other individual. Two relationship combinations that result in conflict are Commander vs. Caregiver and Cheerleader vs. Computer Whiz.

Tip 14: Commander vs. Caregiver Conflict

Commanders, who are fact oriented, direct, and to the point, can come across demanding, blunt, and harsh. The Caregiver, who is focused on feelings and human interaction, will often be offended by that style and take it personally.

One of the ways those two styles can better work together is by compromising. Since the Commander is all fact and no feeling, and the Caregiver is a mostly feeling with no facts, they can create a middle ground if they learn to speak each other's language.

A Commander would benefit from developing empathy and understanding, learning to be more patient and cordial when speaking to the Caregiver.

The Caregiver should think in advance about what he or she wants to say, refrain from getting emotional or taking things personally, and learn to be concise, factual, and to the point in their communication.

Tip 15: Cheerleader vs. Computer Whiz Conflict

The Cheerleader and the Computer Whiz are two personality styles that don't get along well. The Cheerleader is expressive, outgoing and an out-of-the box thinker, while the Computer Whiz is more reserved, introverted, and deals in facts and details.

When a Cheerleader comes in all excited about a new idea they have, the Computer Whiz says to himself or herself, "Get away from me with all that energy." The Cheerleader is hoping the Computer Whiz will relax a little bit and not be so focused on the facts and research.

It's actually in their opposites where they can find common ground. They're extremes on the same spectrum. A Cheerleader should slow down and bring facts to the table, and the Computer Whiz would benefit from taking occasional risks.

Notes

_____

_____

_____

_____

_____

Physiology

"Language is a more recent technology. Your body language, your eyes, your energy will come through to your audience before you even start speaking."

—Peter Guber, Executive Chairman ,Golden State Warriors

Tip 16: How We Say Things

Physiology falls into the category of *how* we say things. Our nonverbal communication (NVC) is an essential part of interpersonal relationships. It's important to understand that the way we express ourselves physically will affect other people. Not all people will always pick up on the nonverbal cues, especially those who lack active listening skills. The two dimensions we explore in nonverbal communication are *visual* and *vocal*.

The visual aspect of communication includes what we observe, such as body language—facial expressions, hand movements, gestures, and posture. We also note presence, use of personal space, touch, energy, and breathing.

The vocal aspect covers tone of a voice, volume, rhythm, and other cues that provide information on the speaker's emotional state and mindset.

Tip 17: Book on the Head

Your posture is the first thing people notice about you. Tall people often tend to come across as more confident and look more powerful, whereas short people have to look up a lot and may not be taken as seriously.

To ensure good posture, create a plumb line. Place your feet shoulder width apart. If you look from a side view, you can draw an imaginary line straight down from the top of your head. Follow through the ear lobe to the shoulder joint, down the center of body (both trunk and abdomen). Continue through the head to the hip bone, down just in front of the center of the knee and through the front of the ankle. Relax your pelvis, flex your abdomen; relax your shoulders as if you're wearing suspenders, and avoid slouching.

For easy visualization, imagine standing with a book on your head.

Tip 18: What's in a Handshake?

For centuries, people have greeted each other by shaking hands. Since as far back as Ancient Greece, the custom of extending your hand when meeting someone was meant to say, "I come in peace, and I am not carrying any weapons in my hands."

A solid, firm handshake shows confidence, as opposed to the "wet fish," which makes you want to wash your hands after meeting someone.

Also, the hand position in a handshake has different nonverbal meanings:

- Positioning your hand from above, as if you were winning an arm wrestling challenge, is a show of dominance and superiority.
- When you meet a person with seniority to you, you might choose to bring your hand from below, as a show of respect.
- A hands position in the center shows that you're approaching the other person as an equal.

Tip 19: Strike a Pose

Different postural poses carry different meaning. While shrugging your shoulders is an obvious clue that you don't have an answer, rounded shoulders show insecurity and lack of confidence.

Leaning from the waist when speaking often happens with headstrong people, who are ready to charge forward in life like a bull. Be mindful, as that posture can be intimidating.

A tip for tall people is to do the following: instead of planting your feet shoulder width apart, bring one leg slightly back, and put your weight on the back leg. You'll appear slightly shorter and less threatening.

The Wonder Woman Power Pose has gained notoriety, thanks to Dr. Amy Cuddy. This is a firm stance, with both feet on the ground, shoulder width apart, and hands on the hips.

The victory pose is another power pose. Imagine a runner crossing the finish line, or a gymnast sticking a landing with both arms in the air, reaching for the sky.

Tip 20: You're in My Space

Have you ever been in a situation where you were uncomfortable because somebody was invading your personal space?

In general, people who are more visual tend to require a larger personal space, and people who are more kinesthetic, the feeler type, will tend to stand closer to others while conversing.

- *Public zone.* The distance you keep from someone at a public event, especially when you don't know the presenter. The distance is 12'–25'.
- *Social zone.* In a business scenario, when you're speaking to a client or team members, this distance is usually 4'–12'.
- *Personal zone.* The distance you keep when speaking to family and friends, which is generally 1'–4'.
- *Intimate zone.* This is the distance reserved for your romantic relationships, typically less than one foot.

We all have our own personal space, so respect others' boundaries.

Tip 21: Where Do You Look?

Imagine yourself in an elevator with a group of people. You're all facing the door, watching the floor numbers change. No one looks at anyone else. Several people get off on the same floor and end up together at a business meeting. It's time for eye contact. Where do you look?

There are three specific gaze regions for eye contact:

- *Business zone.* Form a triangle, where the eyes are the base and the forehead is the tip. Your gaze is from the eyes and above to the forehead.
- *Social zone.* Form a reverse triangle, where the eyes are the base and the mouth is the bottom tip. Your gaze is centered mostly on the nose and cheekbones.
- *Intimate zone.* This is the broadest area, where the eyes are the triangle base and the tip is way down the chest. This is reserved for personal, romantic relationships.

Tip 22: The Eyes Say It All

It's said that "the eyes are the window to the soul." In Western culture, it's customary to make eye contact with people to build trust.

Some reasons why people don't make eye contact include social/cultural differences, nervousness, and shyness.

- Looking away can signify disinterest, while rolling the eyes can mean lack of self-confidence. Pay attention to the individual's body language and demeanor for a complete picture.
- Excessive blinking occurs with stress and tension. From a young age, when we're uncomfortable or nervous, we'll either close our eyes or cover them with our hands.
- Watering eyes shows intense emotion caused by distress or excitement.
- Narrowing of the eyes can show anguish, distress, or anger.
- A glare can be used to intimidate, initiate a challenge, or indicate danger. In males, it may trigger a fight-or-flight response that leads to hormonal release.

Tip 23: Eye Contact— Cultural Exceptions

Different cultures have different rules about eye contact. What might be customary in one society could be considered rude in another.

As previously mentioned, direct eye contact is custom in Western countries, yet in Middle Eastern cultures, it's considered inappropriate for a woman to make eye contact, because such a gesture is seen as romantic. Long, intense eye contact is used to show sincerity and build trust.

In Asian cultures, such as in China and Japan, eye contact in social situations can be deemed inappropriate. Furthermore, subordinates and lower-class individuals shouldn't make eye contact with their superiors. For example, a girl must look down when her father is speaking to her, and students don't look up at their professors, as doing so is a sign of disrespect.

Both African and Latin American cultures still maintain hierarchical social levels. It's considered rude, disrespectful, aggressive, and highly confrontational to look in the eyes of a superior.

Tip 24: If You Just Smile

Nothing breaks the ice as quickly as a smile does. It eases tension and can brighten anyone's day. A smile can make you more likable and approachable. It can make you look younger and more attractive. A nice smile makes you come across trustworthy. To Americans, smiles carry an even deeper meaning, especially if you've got straight teeth when you flash those pearly whites. Americans associate a good smile with being successful, as well as having a good personality.

In addition to giving a personal and social impression, good teeth and a healthy smile can manifest health benefits. Smiling decreases the stress hormones known as cortisol, boosts the immune system, and lowers blood pressure. And the benefits are contagious! Smile, and watch your world change. Smile at others, and see their world change!

Tip 25: Stop Making Faces

Have you ever known people so animated that you knew exactly what they were feeling by looking at their face? Part of your nonverbal communication skill is using your face to express your emotions. We commonly identify seven main types of expressions: happiness, sadness, anger, surprise, fear, disgust, and contempt.

Understanding expressions will help you develop better active listening skills and read the other person's nonverbal cues.

Two categories of facial expressions include the following:

- *Macro expressions* are obvious and easily detected. We most use these expressions when we're alone, or with friends and family, and feel comfortable.
- *Micro expressions* are short versions of the macro expressions, and they represent hidden emotions you're attempting to conceal. Your subconscious fires so quickly that you won't be able to hide them completely.

Use the following chart, and focus on the differences in the forehead, brow, eyes, nose, and mouth to familiarize yourself with the expressions.

Tip 26: Are You Flailing Your Arms?

Use of the arms is extremely important in communication. Whether speaking one-on-one or presenting in front of a group, arm movement will add to the conversation dynamics and help clarify the message. When in front of a group, use larger gestures from the shoulder rather than from the elbow. This way, you won't look like a penguin.

There are two zones for arm gestures. Your upper chest and heart region are considered your *passion zone*. Your midsection is considered your *trust zone*.

To be inviting, always keep your gestures in an open position. Refrain from putting your arms behind your back. Crossing your arms over your chest might be done for comfort, but this can be seen as erecting a protective barrier. Keeping your arms in front of you delivers the nonverbal message that you're trustworthy and have nothing to hide.

Tip 27: Wave Like the Queen

Here are common hand gestures and their meanings:

- Palms up—I come in peace
- Palms down—I give you orders
- Rubbing your hands together—Shows excitement
- Clasping your hands together—Shows frustration and holding back
- Cupping fingers—Driving home the point
- Thumbs up or down—In ancient days was to either spare or execute a gladiator
- Rubbing the back of the neck—Shows discomfort, or subconscious sign that someone is being a pain in the neck
- Scratching the head—I don't know
- Rubbing in your ear—Wanting to block out the sound
- Covering your mouth—Stopping your words
- Pointing, finger batons, and karate chops—All can indicate disagreement and/or displeasure

- Fidgeting—Performing isolated, repetitive gestures, which shows stress, worry, or boredom

Notes

_____

_____

_____

_____

_____

_____

_____

_____

_____

_____

_____

_____

_____

_____

_____

Tip 28: Where Does Your Voice Live?

You can project your vocal power from three regions—the chest, head, or middle—to give a different quality and presence.

To exhibit a dominant voice, which relates to leadership, assertiveness, and security, use a more expressive voice, resonating primarily in the chest area, with an upbeat tone.

- A *chest voice* comes from the diaphragm, has deep resonance, and cuts through loud environments. Practice saying, "AAAAA," put your hand on your chest, and feel the vibration.

- A lightweight, submissive, melodic voice shows uncertainty, doubt, and passivity. Your voice sounds more somber and softer, and comes from the head region. Its quality is thin, nasally, and sounds like yelling. Over time, it can damage your vocal cords.

- A *head voice* resonates at the front of your nose. Practicing the letters M, N, and NG brings vibration to the front of your face.

- A *middle voice* combines both regions and is great for speaking and singing.

Use head voice for soft speaking and whispering

Tip 29: Take a Breath

Back in high school, while I was singing a solo at an event, the microphone lost power. I was on stage, with 1,000 people in the audience. What do I do? I remember taking a deep breath and using the air in my lungs to move the sound through, hoping it would reach the back row. To my surprise, it did.

Most people breathe through their chest and don't get enough air in their lungs. Proper breathing is done by using your diaphragm. Inhale through your nose, and imagine you're inflating a balloon in your abdomen. Let it relax and expand. Exhale through your mouth. Keep your shoulder and neck muscles relaxed.

Wait until you fully inhale before you start speaking. Slowly use the breath to let your words flow through. Use less breath when whispering and more breath to project your voice.

Download a great breathing exercise at https://drkarenjacobson.com/freebies/

Tip 30: Practice Vocal Variety

A string quartet is comprised of a violin, viola, cello, and bass. They all have a similar structure, yet differ in sizes and sound.

Your voice is your instrument, allowing you to express emotions, capture attention, and command a room. Using vocal variety in tempo, volume, pitch, and resonance is important.

Tempo is important in an expressive voice. Play with tempo and change the pace, moving from slow to fast and fast to slow. Slow is used for emphasis, whereas fast can be used for excitement and humor.

Raising the volume or lowering it, changing the pitch and resonance, will add dimension. Bring in a fullness of emotion—delight, joy, sorrow, disgust. Yes, even the negative emotions.

Changes in volume can be used to make a point. When changing the topic, pause and change your voice.

Tip 31: Protecting Your Voice

Your voice is a precious instrument that allows you to express emotions, connect with people, and build relationships. When you strive to communicate effectively, it's imperative to protect your voice, especially if you're using it for presentations.

Here are some quick tips that can help you protect your vocal chords and voice:

1. Practice deep breathing, with the diaphragm and pelvis.
2. Embrace body relaxation—correct posture is the key. Reduce shoulder, neck, and throat tension. Do facial relaxation exercises and musical scales.
3. Cleanse and condition, by gargling with a mixture of warm water, a teaspoon of salt, and baking soda. Follow up with hot herbal tea and honey.
4. Before a presentation or speech, as well as during an event, stay hydrated to avoid fatigue and damage.

5. Protect your voice by eating balanced meals, getting plenty of rest, and avoiding smoky areas.

Ready to step outside the box? Take voice lessons to increase your effectiveness.

Tip 32: Oops, I Did It Again

The way you use your voice can make or break you. Just as you can build credibility through good habits, you can destroy your image using bad habits.

Bad vocal habits to avoid:

- Speaking with a nasally, whiny, crying voice that extends to your words. This makes you appear weak and powerless.
- Using a breathy voice, like Marilyn Monroe is appropriate for the bedroom, not the boardroom.
- Vocal fry (think Kim Kardashian or Britney Spears)—speaking below the normal register in a cracking, gravely sound—takes away your power.
- Shrilling, speaking at a high, almost screechy tone, denotes nervousness.
- Uptalk is signified by raising your pitch at the end of a sentence, as if you're asking a question. This will make you come across as unsure of yourself. Uptalk is more common in women. A statement should end on an even or slightly lower pitch.

Tip 33: Great Color for You!

First rule: know your audience. Are they corporate or entrepreneurs? Are they conservative, liberal, or free-spirited? Match your attire to the audience, and choose your colors for individuality and the nature of your message.

- Black—power, authority, and strength.
- White—open, safe, righteous.
- Blue—safe for men and women, establishes trust and credibility, also symbolizes communication. Dark blue or dark gray are conservative, professional, and authoritative.
- Royal blue, blue-green, and teal—friendly, approachable, show confidence, and high self-esteem; the same applies to tan and peachy-orange.
- Red—great for the stage or a large group talk. Can be intimidating in some circles.
- Green—dependability and emotional balance. Not always a crowd favorite.
- Gray or Beige—neutral colors allowing your personality to shine through, though you might come across a bit dull or as a people pleaser, saying what people want to hear.

- Magenta—shock, inspire your audience!
- Purple—royalty and wealth

Notes

_____

_____

_____

_____

_____

_____

_____

_____

_____

_____

_____

_____

_____

_____

Phraseology

"Words mean more than what is set down on paper. It takes the human voice to infuse them with deeper meaning."

—Maya Angelou

Tip 34: What We Say

An old childhood saying goes, "Sticks and stones may break my bones, but words will never hurt me." In the past, the belief was to ignore what was being said, but we now understand the effect that language has, specifically on the subconscious. Ask anyone who's been bullied.

According to Sigmund Freud 1915 your subconscious houses your emotions and takes everything personally. It responds to clear, sequential orders, it controls 97% of your perceptions and behavior, and its job is to protect you at all times from any threats or danger (e.g., the fight-or-flight response).

Therefore, words do have meaning and carry weight. They can either build you up or tear you down. Create trust or destroy it. Choosing the right words, especially in difficult situations, can help you build bridges, calm people down, and build relationships.

Tip 35: How Your Language Trips You

1. *Negative self-talk.* What are you saying to yourself? Is your language empowering or disempowering? Negative self-talk will affect not only the way you see the world, but also the way others see you.
2. *Lack of clarity and using "fluff."* Why use a sentence when you can say the same thing in one or two words? Unless you're painting a picture, simple, direct communication will eliminate redundancy.
3. *Saying too much.* Less is more. Make your words easy, short, and to the point.
4. *Getting too technical.* Avoid jargon, especially when talking to nontechnical people.
5. *Body language incongruent with words.* People can read the subtle, nonverbal communication cues, and it happens on a subconscious level. Those incongruences will cause us to break rapport, develop suspicion, and lack of trust in people.

Tip 36: Stop Words and Fillers

What you say can change people's reactions and lives. While it's important to know what to say, it's also important to know what not to say.

Language fillers and repeated words such as "ah," "um," "mark my words," "don't you worry about that," and so forth denote hesitancy and decrease credibility.

Along with your words being congruent with your ideas, your words and nonverbal communication should also be congruent.

Stop words create a barrier with your listeners. Here are stop words to avoid:

- "No, I agree." Which one is it? The minute you say "no," you break the rapport with the person you're speaking to. Replace this statement with "Yes, I agree."
- "I agree, but ..." The minute you say "but," you negate everything you've said prior to that moment. Instead say, "I agree, and ..."

Speaking in a clear, concise, precise manner allows you to be an effective communicator.

Tip 37: Open Mouth, Insert Foot

Have you ever found yourself in a situation where you started speaking, and before you even finished talking you wish you'd never opened your mouth?

Being able to think on your feet is a skill that you can develop. Here are some things to think about before you speak:

1. Act as an observer in a conversation, and practice active listening skills. Pay attention to what is being said and watch the nonverbal cues.

2. What's your goal for the conversation? Are you looking to be effective, to provide accurate and timely advice or something meaningful? Or are you just looking to be heard?

3. Notice if anything said in the conversation sets you off and hits any of your buttons.

4. Once it's your turn to respond, take a breath and pause momentarily. Think about what you want to say, how you will

say it, and why it's important, valuable, and timely.

Listen - Pause -Think - Speak

Tip 38: The Sound of Silence

You walk into a room, and you notice a couple of people sitting there silently. The tension is awkward. The silence might be a result of conflict or discomfort. But that's not the type of silence I'm referring to.

Another negative way to use silence is when giving someone the silent treatment. That type of passive-aggressive behavior is not being encouraged here.

Under the right circumstances, when used positively, silence is a powerful communication tool.

When you're asked a question, silence offers you the opportunity to compose your thoughts. Take a moment, repeat the question in your mind, figure things out, and decide what you want to say.

Silence also allows other people to compose their thoughts. Some people need more time to process information. Having silence provides space and prevents you from coming across as pushy.

Notes

_____

_____

_____

_____

_____

_____

_____

_____

_____

_____

_____

_____

_____

_____

_____

_____

_____

Inner Conversations

*"If you hear a voice within
you say 'you cannot paint,'
then by all means paint, and
that voice will be silenced."*

—Vincent Van Gogh

Tip 39: Quiet Your Inner Critic

How many times have you found yourself in a conversation where you were self-criticizing and spewing negativity about your own behavior?

None of us enjoy when other people put down our work or have something negative to say about the way we've conducted ourselves.

What about when that someone is your own inner voice? The small voice inside, your inner critic, plays a major role in how you show up with other people.

Your outer world reflects your internal conversation. It sets the tone for how you communicate with other people and how you show up in the world.

If you continuously beat yourself down, criticize yourself, and dwell in negativity, the first impression you make on other people will be far from positive.

Keep your internal conversation positive. Words have power—they will impact your life!

Tip 40: I Won't Back Down

Have you ever had a conversation with yourself, attempting to motivate yourself to doing something you were procrastinating getting done?

You must have a reason to do what you do. Whenever you're asked to act, your mind asks WIIFM: what's in it for me? In other words, why should I do this?

It all boils down to having a compelling reason. In his book *Start with Why*, Simon Sinek talks about discovering your Why.

Knowing your Why provides the ability to design the process of how you can be motivated. Whether self-motivation or encouragement from an outside source, there must be a good reason and a personal benefit. It's the way we're wired.

When you tie your goals to your Why, they'll have more power, and you'll be internally motivated to take action and chances.

Tip 41: You or I?

"You were late giving me the info I needed, which made me late in sending the offer. Now I might lose the deal because of that." Does pointing a finger at someone really help the situation?

There are specific times when you want to speak from the first person, using "I."

Speak from the "I" when you're focused on establishing rapport, especially when you're planning to confront someone in a challenging situation.

Take ownership of your feelings (loving honesty), and stay in the "I" language to express your feelings, as opposed to "you" conversation, which is finger pointing and puts your listener on the defensive.

You may have references to "I" in your sales when establishing credibility. But then shift to the benefits your reader or listener will experience. That's a perfect time to use second person, "you" conversation

Notes

_____

_____

Power Conversations

*"Speech is power:
speech is to persuade, to
convert, to compel. It is
to bring another out of
his bad sense into your
good sense."*

—Ralph Waldo Emerson

Tip 42: Show Up Strong

In *The Devil Wears Prada*, Meryl Streep plays the mean boss that everyone hates and fears. Aggressive behavior is definitely not the way to win friends and influence people.

When you want to show up strong, adopt an assertive approach rather than an aggressive one.

- Being assertive means showing up in your power, rather than using force.
- Being assertive means you know who you are and what your boundaries are, rather than have an inflated self-image.
- Being assertive means you know what you're asking for, and you keep your responses short, rather than demanding what you want and rambling on and on.
- Being assertive means you deepen your voice when speaking, slow your pace, and maintain your calm, rather than raising your voice, getting worked up, and speaking too quickly.
- Being assertive means you respect when people say, "no," rather than keep on pushing and getting angry.

Tip 43: Have Some Empathy

We're told we don't know what someone else is going through until we walk a mile in his or her shoes. The truth is, no matter what we've been through in our own lives, we can never experience someone else's feelings. What we can do is have compassion when people are facing a challenge.

Some of you might be thinking, "They always have drama. I have no patience for this. I can't be walking on eggshells or coddling them." You don't need to take on their story, prove its validity, or identify with it. Taking on someone's issue, "feeling their pain," feeling sorry for them, and/or trying to fix things is sympathy, not empathy.

Having some empathy toward another human being who's struggling is part of human kindness. A little understanding can go a long way.

Tip 44: Remember My Name

You're at a business event, and from across the room, someone walks up to you with a big smile on his or her face. "I can't believe you're here. So great to see you! It's been such a long time." You smile, nodding, thinking, "I know the face. I know I've met them, and for the life of me I can't remember this person's name." Your coworker walks up and says, "Will you introduce me to your friend?"

Names and faces. Many say they forget names but will never forget a face. People will feel good when you remember their names. Here are three tips to help you with that:

- When meeting a new person, repeat his or her name slowly, say it at least twice.
- Find something unique about the person and connect the name to it—for example, smiling Sam or dancing Diane.
- Create an association with someone else who has the same/a similar name. Ex. I always remember every Lisa I meet since it's the same name as my sister.

Most importantly, BE PRESENT!

Tip 45: From Their Perspective

Whether in selling or networking, we approach people based on our perceptions, experiences, and beliefs. Ask the average salesperson what his or her selling strategy is, and you'll get a rundown of the process used with everyone.

In high-performance communication our goal is to create powerful conversations and build rapport with people. If you were visiting a foreign country, wouldn't you learn how to speak the language?

Here are examples of three questions to make your listener feel comfortable, and to gather information in the process:

- When approaching someone for a face-to-face or phone conversation, ask, "Is this a good time for you?"
- When scheduling a meeting, provide a couple of time options and ask, "What works best for you, morning or afternoon?"
- When explaining a concept, assigning tasks, explaining an issue, or making

a sale, follow up by asking, "What questions do you have?"

Don't force your agenda on others, ask to be invited in

Tip 46: I'm Right, You're Wrong

"Anything you can do I can do better. I can do anything better than you!" While that might have been considered cute in 1946 on Broadway, it doesn't fly when it comes to high-performance communication.

A certain amount of competition is healthy. However, the concept of "one-upping" another will cause people to walk away from you.

People who need to be right are generally insecure and/or perfectionists. Leave room for other people to have their opinions.

The need to dominate conversations comes from a power struggle. Let other people speak; you're not alone in the room. Dominate, and you might be.

Pointing out when someone is wrong and/or shaming people serves no purpose. Let people have their dignity.

Avoid telling people how they should feel. Everyone perceives things differently. Own your feelings; they own theirs.

Tip 47: You Done Good

What's the best way to empower your team members? Praise them! When you praise someone for a job well done, you're reinforcing a pattern of good behavior.

Our actions are built on habits. Every habit has a trigger, an action, and a reward. The best way to praise someone is to do it immediately. Direct your comment to the specific action the person has taken and reinforce the positive outcome that resulted.

For example, you might say, "Deanna, I wanted to let you know how pleased I am with the report you submitted. I really appreciate all the research you did. Great job!"

Praise creates positive effects on the listener, resulting in a release of dopamine, also known as the happy hormone. That feeling is the reward that anchors the behavior in the listener, and they're likely to repeat it in the future.

Tip 48: Mastering Persuasion

Have you ever had an idea that has met with resistance? The answer might have been right in front of you, but you knew that if you told someone what to do, they wouldn't embrace the action? There's a better way. When an individual reaches a conclusion on his or her own and chooses an action or embraces an idea, that person also has buy in.

The Socratic method stimulates critical thinking and helps you influence and persuade through questions and logic. Here are different types of questions you can ask to reach the desired outcome:

- Questions to help clarify the meaning of what someone says
- Questions that help explain the rationale, evidence, and logic someone is using
- Questions to substantiate individual viewpoints and opinions
- Questions that get to the root cause of others' questions

Notes

_____

_____

_____

_____

_____

_____

_____

_____

_____

_____

_____

_____

_____

_____

_____

_____

_____

_____

Tip 49: Let's Negotiate

From deciding where to eat lunch to big business decisions, negotiations are part of our daily lives. Some cultures thrive on negotiation but handle such situations differently.

In a collaborative business, the ideal outcome of a negotiation is a win-win. Keep in mind the following to achieve that goal:

- Decide what your end goal is. Know your audience, their culture and values.
- If possible, meet face to face. Use a round table or positioned seats at a 90° angle to each other, respecting personal space.
- Find commonalities for agreement points.
- Control the negotiation. Be the one asking the questions and leading the pace, while mirroring and matching.
- With all four stages of selling— prospects, qualify, present, and close— the presentation is the most important. Focus on the benefits of the benefits.
- Prepare second options.
- Silence can give you an edge—use it.

Tip 50: Tips for a Successful Job Interview

1. Prepare in advance. Have a clean copy of your résumé and the proper outfit ready the night before.
2. Read up on the company; understand its culture and mission.
3. Arrive early.
4. Practice your handshake technique—telescope your handshake (i.e., reach forward as you walk).
5. Be confident, but not overpowering, and smile.
6. When possible, sit somewhere other than the opposite side of the desk. If not, sit slightly angled, so you're not in a defensive position.
7. Maintain an open posture, sit up straight, and refrain from fidgeting.
8. Mirror and match to build rapport.
9. When referring to your résumé, use a pen to guide the eyes. See if you can have the interviewer approach you and sit beside you, if there's an open seat.

10. When the interview ends, shake hands to say goodbye. Show the same confidence you did as when you entered.

Notes

_____

_____

_____

_____

_____

_____

_____

_____

_____

_____

_____

_____

_____

_____

Tip 51: My Generation

Clarence and Kyle work in the same company. Clarence is upset because he's left several voice messages for Kyle, but Kyle hasn't responded. As a matter of fact, Kyle rarely answers his phone. He does use his phone for work on a regular basis, but to text and send email. When Clarence confronted Kyle, he said, "Just text me." Sound familiar?

With five generations in the workplace, it has been increasingly difficult to bridge some communication gaps—different communication modes, different work ethics, and different values.

A simple question to ask coworkers is, "What is the best way to reach you?"

Use the following as a general reference:

- Traditionalists and baby boomers—call them
- Gen Xers—email them
- Millennials and Generations Z—text them

Approach them in their preferred communication mode, and then ask them to reciprocate in yours.

Tip 52: C.A.L.M. for Conflict Resolution, Part 1

Have you ever had to diffuse an argument at work or talk someone off an emotional cliff? It's not unusual that when someone yells at you, it pushes your buttons. While you might be tempted to react in a similar fashion, you'll only add fuel to the fire with that kind of reaction. When most people are stressed and express anger, they just want to be heard, acknowledged, and validated. Do exactly that. Validate their feelings, then implement a method of conflict resolution and emotional deescalation, the Four-Step C.A.L.M. Process:

C - Create Clarity

A - Acknowledge and Accept

L - Listen and Look

M - Mutual Respect

Tip 53: C.A.L.M. for Conflict Resolution, Part 2

C - Create Clarity around facts and find out the cause of the anger and emotional upset.

Once you validate their feelings, this will help deescalate the conflict. Be sure to focus on the facts only, not feelings. Handle the conversation in private, to respect the individual. If the outburst occurs during a meeting, acknowledge the issue but defer the conversation until later, out of respect for the team. If you're in private an example of what you might say to that situation is, "I can see that this is an issue. What exactly happened to cause the problem?"

In public you would say." I can see that this is an issue. How about we discuss this immediately right after the meeting" Then proceed with the rest of the process in private.

A - Acknowledge and Accept, being tolerant and accepting different opinions.

L - Listen and Look, discovering similarities to help you establish common ground for agreement.

M- Mutual Respect should always be expressed, whether in reaching a beneficial compromise or agreeing to disagree.

Tip 54: Dealing with a Loss

One of the most difficult conversations is speaking to someone who has just experienced a personal loss, was fired from his or her job, has gone through a breakup, or has been given a life-altering diagnosis.

What do you say?

Often people will say something like "I feel your pain" or "I understand what you're going through." Then they proceed to talk about their own experience. Unfortunately, that takes the focus off the individual and, in all honesty, is far from comforting. Basically, two strikes against them. Regardless of our experience, we can never truly know what someone else is going through.

The best thing you can do is say the following: "What do you need?" or "How can I support you through this difficult time?" Let the individual tell you exactly what he or she needs or wants.

Tip 55: Stop Babysitting

In today's business world, an open-door policy is a common management practice. Our goal is to keep the communication lines open and show our availability.

By the same token, *Leadership Quarterly* states research that shows that 42% of managers' time is spent on conflict resolution—in other words, handholding and babysitting.

When Claire walks into your office telling you that she's had it with Timothy, and she can't work with him anymore because he's being uncooperative, what do you do?

Begin by listening to her, and getting the facts. She'll feel valued. Your next step is to empower her to handle the conflict on her own, by asking, "What did Timothy say when you spoke to him about the issue?" She probably hasn't spoken with Timothy, so role-play some possible conversations with him.

Finally, ask, "When would be a good time to check back with you?" and send her on her way.

Tip 56: Taking the High Road

Your colleague walks into your office, complaining about another coworker. He or she begins talking about a personal incident that happened between the two of them, and then started gossiping and badmouthing the coworker. What do you do?

In high-performance communication, integrity is a core value. Mouth management is essential. We all know there's no room at work for gossip or badmouthing a colleague, but does our behavior reflect that? It's quite easy to get caught up in a conversation and gossip.

Think of it this way: what if the roles were reversed, and the colleague and other coworker were badmouthing and gossiping about you?

Here is what you can say: "I'm sorry you had that experience. As far as the rest, it sounds like its [Name's] personal business, and I'm not sure he/she would want me to know about it, so let's not discuss it."

Notes

_____

_____

_____

Non-Face-to-Face Communication

"Write to be understood, speak to be heard, read to grow."

—Lawrence Clark Powell

Tip 57: Hey, Hey Telephone Line

Unless you're on a video conference, the phone removes the visual aspect of communication, and you must rely on your other senses, such as vocal and verbal, to gain information about the person you're speaking to. Pay attention to tone, pitch, volume, and other vocal cues to help you detect the person's mood and personality. Are they excited, stressed, or angry? Picking up on the auditory cues will help you relate to the individual. On your end, to exude confidence during the call, your best strategy is to stand during the conversation. Standing will help you keep your energy high and your voice strong. In addition, be sure to smile, which will help you come across as friendly. Even though the listener cannot see you, they'll actually know whether you're smiling or not.

Be polite and respectful, and keep your language clean when asking for something.

Tip 58: Your Email DON'Ts

The following email habits can get you into trouble, so be sure to avoid them.

- Don't write in all caps or in bold. You'll be perceived as yelling at your reader.
- Don't use "Re." in your email header, to make it seem as though you're responding to the person's email.
- Don't hit "reply all," and don't carbon copy (cc) or blind copy (bcc) people who have no reason to be included in the email.
- Don't write long emails; they won't be read.
- Don't use jargon or technical terminology in an email intended for general audience.
- Don't use emoji in your professional emails, especially not when representing the business.
- Don't make common spelling mistakes that affect your credibility (e.g., they're vs. their vs. there; your vs. you're; its vs. it's; affect vs. effect; into vs. in to).

What are some of your email pet peeves?

_____

_____

_____

_____

_____

_____

_____

_____

Tip 59: Your Email DO's

A business email is a public and legal document. The way you present yourself can have a major effect on your professional image. Be mindful of the way you write, your tone and your grammar.

- If you want the reader to open your email, use a short, to the point subject, to grab the recipient's attention. Be clear, concise, and precise in your email, and use bullet points and short paragraphs.
- Send your email only to those who are relevant. When you have multiple recipients, use the blind carbon copy feature (bcc), unless company policy is different.
- Use professional-casual language. Edit and proofread your email for grammar and content.
- Be polite and respectful when asking for something, and keep your language clean.

Tip 60: Clear, Concise Email

Now that we've discussed overall good and bad email habits, let's talk about content. Since an email is intended to deliver a clear, concise, and precise message, how do we write it?

Consider that your audience consists of mixed communication styles—Commanders, Cheerleaders, Caregivers, and Computer Whizzes. They need the Who, What, Why, and How.

Think about the information you're delivering, and ask yourself the following questions:

- *Who* needs to know this information? Who is this for? That's how you pick your recipients.
- *What* is the big idea I need to deliver? That's your subject.
- *Why* is it important and what is the purpose for this correspondence? Is it to inform others, take action, ask for reply, etc.?
- *How* is this going to happen? This would be provide some details of the process.
- Depending on the subject, you might add in a *When* and *Where*.

By covering all those points and sticking to facts, you answer everyone's questions.

Notes

_____

_____

_____

_____

_____

_____

_____

_____

_____

_____

_____

_____

_____

Networking

"Effective networking isn't a result of luck—it requires hard work and persistence."

—Lewis Howes

Tip 61: The Power of a First Impression

With the rise of the technology age and social media, it's a known fact that people's attention spans have shortened. It's said that it only takes up to 7 seconds to make a first impression. Your first impression can make or break you, so you need to make every second count. People observe your energy, the way you carry yourself, your clothing, demeanor, and words.

Do the following to increase your impact from the first minute:

1. Dress the part; be professional.
2. Have a good, strong handshake.
3. Introduce yourself clearly, and ask the other person's name; repeat it.
4. Maintain appropriate eye contact, without staring.
5. Smile like you mean it, with your eyes.

The right first impression can and lead to a long-lasting connection.

Tip 62: Rules of Engagement, Part 1

Establish Contact. Whether at a meeting, conference, or networking event, the first step is to establish contact with another person. While not all people are comfortable with walking up to a stranger to start a conversation, a smile and eye contact can serve as ice breakers that ease the tension. How do you decide who to walk up to at an event?

_____

_____

_____

Create Curiosity. Build rapport by creating a little mystique. It's all in what questions you choose to ask and the topics you discuss. Some people are better than others at small talk. You can begin a conversation by giving someone a compliment, noticing a unique tie, watch, or piece of jewelry. Be prepared by picking some topics you can use when meeting new people.

_____

_____

_____

Tip 63: Rules of Engagement, Part 2

Develop a Connection. Once you've made the initial contact and piqued the person's curiosity, you're on the right track. Now you have to deepen the conversation, which you can do by asking open-ended questions that make the person feel valued. The best questions are those that provide you with information about the individual, his or her needs and challenges, while also helping you establish a strong rapport.

CTA, Your Call to Action. When meeting new people, it's always important to figure out your next step. Are you looking for a further connection, or will the conversation end right there? If you have no interest, thank the individual for his or her time, and move on to the next person. If you see possibility for collaboration or synergy, exchange cards and invite the person to continue the conversation either online or in person. The quality of your connections is key!

Tip 64: What's a Networking Buddy?

There's power in numbers, yet not in the way you might think. It's not about collecting business cards—it's about strategy. Partner with a colleague as a Networking Buddy.

Three benefits to a Networking Buddy include the following:

- You can walk around and feel comfortable joining in a group, especially if one of you is more of an introvert. There's no need to worry about walking into an event solo, feeling uneasy joining other people in a conversation.
- You know different people, and you can increase your sphere of influence by introducing each other to your connections.
- You can use your buddy to promote each other to new people. When somebody else promotes you, this enhances your credibility and serves as a testimonial to your work.

Tip 65: Follow up, Don't Spam

You're back from your event. You have a handful of cards from a group of new people. What are the do's and don'ts for successful follow up?

How often have you met someone at an event, who then connected with you online, immediately added you to their mailing list, and started selling to you?

Did you like that? Don't do that to others! It's a sure way to lose both connections and credibility.

Since we're dealing with business, go straight to LinkedIn® and invite them to your network. When you send the invitation, ad a personal note reminding the person about where and when you met. If you think there's potential synergy, offer to connect through a conference call, on a platform like Skype™ or Zoom. If the person is local, have lunch or coffee with him or her. Respect your connections. You never know who they might know.

Notes

_____

_____

_____

_____

_____

_____

_____

_____

_____

_____

_____

_____

_____

_____

_____

When you align your intention with your expression, you leave a lasting impression.

—Dr. Karen Jacobson

Final Thoughts

Congratulations—you've done it!

I hope you take advantage of the tips in this book. The great news about communication skills is that you can master them if you choose to do so. Communication is a two-way street. A great way to uplevel your skill sets is to share this book with a friend and practice the tips. The more you practice, the more good habits you'll create. Set aside time to practice—put it on your schedule, and commit to your success.

If you would like to take this to the next level perhaps consider a live training. There are several programs in the High-Performance Triad series that I customize to the needs of your team and your company to help you elevate your skills to the next level.

Uplevel your communication
Uplevel your game
Uplevel your success!

About The Author

Dr. Karen Jacobson, High-Performance Strategist, Speaker

Israeli Military Commander. Doctor. Champion Ballroom Dancer. What these have in common isn't the *what*, it's the *who*. Dr. Karen Jacobson integrates her diverse background into her personal brand as a keynote speaker at state and national conferences and corporate events, including team training.

With more than 30 years of training experience, Dr. Karen mesmerizes audiences with her high-caliber presentation style, while relating her groundbreaking framework regarding communication in the face of adversity, based on her experiences with arduous military training, then later as an award-winning ballroom dancer.

As an expert in communication, Dr. Karen Jacobson is the creator of the "**High-Performance Triad**," a trademark-pending, effective strategy for creating YOUR highest edge. Your audience and teams will leave energized and armed with an arsenal of new skill sets and tools, to provide lasting transformation.

To book Dr. Jacobson to speak at your next event or for information about her High-Performance Programs, visit www.drkarenjacobson.com or email her at admin@drkarenjacobson.com.

Connect with Dr. Karen Jacobson on social media:

https://www.linkedin.com/in/drkarenjacobson/
https://www.facebook.com/DrKarenJacobson/
https://twitter.com/DrKarenJacobson
https://www.youtube.com/c/DrKarenJacobson
https://plus.google.com/+DrKarenJacobson

Made in the USA
Middletown, DE
29 July 2022

70173023R00066